"Wiggles," Stomps and Squeezes

Calming my Jitters at School

LINDSEY ROWE PARKER

Illustrated by
REBECCA BURGESS

Published in the United States by BQB Publishing
(an imprint of Boutique of Quality Books Publishing Company)
www.bqbpublishing.com

9798886330212 (hc)
9798886330229 (e)

Library of Congress Control Number: 2023946266

Cover and interior illustrations: Rebecca Burgess
Interior Design Setup: Robin Krauss, www.bookformatters.com
Editor: Andrea Berns

Praise for Wiggles, Stomps, and Squeezes

"As the parent of an autistic Kindergartener, this book is essential in our home! The words and images are deeply immersive, transporting me into my son's sensory experiences in a way that no other book has done. The story normalizes and validates sensory needs and models practical, affirming ways to meet them. Most importantly, though, my son truly sees himself in this book, and this representation has impacted him powerfully. Books like this one give me hope for a more inclusive world."

   – Ellie Hunja, author of Blessings, New Mom

"In all my years teaching, I have never come across a more accurate representation of my students' unique sensory needs while at school. This book will give all students who need to wiggle, stomp, and squeeze a boost in confidence."

   – Stephanie Bolin, Special Education Teacher

"As a licensed therapist specializing in working from a neurodiversity-affirming lens, this book has so much to offer to kids and adults of all neurotypes and provides much needed representation to kids who have sensory and movement needs! I love that this book normalizes using stimming, movement, and sensory experiences to help regulate at school. It's so special to read a story that highlights what a day can look like when a child is having their needs accommodated and validated by other people in their environment."

   – Brittany Ashmore, M.S., LMFT (Licensed Marriage and Family Therapist)

Dedications

To those who embrace every child just as they are, and come alongside them as they learn and grow. Thank you.

– Lindsey

For Holly, Thank you for being there beside me in every new journey I take.

xxxx – Bex

I need to *wiggle*, I need to **spin!**

I can't explain why.

1

"Today is a schoooooool day, schooool day," Mom sings.
She takes my hand and we spin, spin, spin around.
She makes me giggle with her goofy songs.

"What would you like to
wear today?" she asks.

3

I want my favorite shirt,
the one with the dinosaur.

I point to it, it's in
the stinky pile.

"Hmm, can we try the shirt with the planets
today? That one is clean, and we'll get
the dino shirt washed for tomorrow."

4

I feel my jitters
start to bubble inside.
Little bubbles, like the kind
in orange soda.

5

She shows me the shirt with the planets.
They have sparkles and they match my shoes.
I nod. I do like planets. Especially Jupiter.
It's my favorite.

She takes my hand and we

spin,
spin,
spin,
around.

That's what calms
my jitters down.

7

I need to wiggle, I need to hum! I can't explain why.
The kids bounce up and down
in their seats. Their heads bobble as
we rumble down the street.

8

The sound of the engine
is loud in my ears.
I cover them and
my jitters come back.

9

I look out the window. The school is
teeny tiny and gets bigger and bigger
as we get closer and closer.

"Almost there. I am loving your planet shirt!"
the bus driver says.

His smile is familiar and kind.

12

I need to march, I need to tap! I can't explain why.
The classroom is bright and noisy.
Chattering voices float all around me.

14

My desk is smooth and cool.
I place my palms down on it,
and my cheek.

I **tap-tap-tap** my fingers
one by one by one.

There is a scratch on the edge of my desk.
I run my finger along the bumpy side
to the smooth side and back again.

"Let's get our pencils out. We're going to do a worksheet," the teacher says to the class.

16

I look at the paper in her hand. The words are squiggly. And squiggly words feel loud, even when no one is talking. I feel my jitters come back. The bubbles are bigger this time.

I **tap-tap-tap** my pencil
on the desk, making sure
to avoid the scratch.

18

My teacher sees my tapping.
"Do you want to help me pass these out?" she asks.

I jump from my seat.
I am great at helping!

She hands me the stack.
I am very careful
not to bend the pages.

I march around the room
in a biiiiig circle
like an orbit and I'm a planet.
I'm Jupiter. It's my favorite.

20

I hand each of my friends
a paper one by one by one.
"Thank you!" they say. I smile
and march, march, march.
And it calms my jitters down.

21

I need to zoom, I need to climb! I can't explain why.
The ladder is cold on my hands as I pull myself to the top.

22

Up, up, up I go. My friends look like teeny tiny ants. I stay above for a while until someone shouts for their turn.

23

I'm not ready yet.
The slide is fast. I want to be ready.

I can see the moon. Maybe I can see the planets from up here?

They shout again.
My jitters come back.

25

I point my feet toward the
ground and push off.

who

I am weightless.
Zooming down toward
the ground.

I shriek. My voice
is loud inside my head.

oosh!

My shoes hit the ground.
It shakes beneath my feet. I've got to do that again.
I climb up, up, up! And it calms my jitters down.

I need to stomp, I need to move!
I can't explain why.

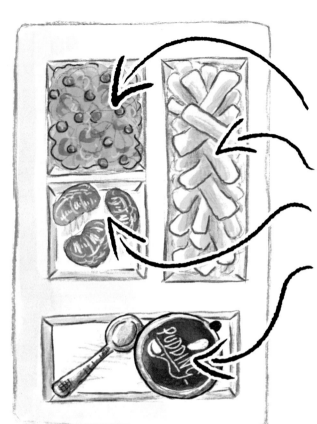

I look at the tray of food in front of me. I inspect each item—

something **squishy**,
something **crusty**,
something **juicy**,
something **gooey**...

My tummy growls and my jitters come back.

I stick my spoon into my chocolate pudding. It's gooey, but I do like chocolate.

29

I stick my
tongue out to taste.

YIKES!

The spoon slips out of my hand! It rolls down my shirt and pants and onto my sparkly shoes!

Oh noooo, pudding has squished onto Jupiter!

31

OK, OK. I wipe it off with my hand, but it smears it more.

The brown, gooey pudding has covered my planets!

32

Arrrrrrghhh!

I roar!

I need my dinosaur shirt! Dinosaurs love mud.
They can be gooey, but not Jupiter! Jupiter is NOT gooey.

I growl and shove my tray away. Dinosaurs do not like squishy food!
I don't need squishy food! Dinosaurs need to stomp!

My jitters are bubbling over! Like lava from a volcano!
My face is hot. I can feel my friends looking at me.

Crunch, Crunch, Crunch.

My lava begins to cool.
"I hear dinosaurs love crunchy foods," my teacher says.

She shares some of her favorite "dino snacks'" with me and finds me a spare shirt.

She puts my planets in a special take-home bag to keep them safe. The sparkles are not sparkling and Jupiter is still gooey and brown, but I put it in my backpack. She says we can fix it.

I take a Dee

38

eeeP breath. My tummy feels a bit better.
And my dinosaur has stopped roaring.

Crunch, crunch, crunch.
That's what calms my jitters down.

I need a squish, I need a squeeze!
I can't explain why.
My planets with the gooey
pudding are in the stinky pile.

40

My clean dino shirt is folded on
my bed. "It's ready for a new adventure,"
Dad says. I can't wait to wear it tomorrow.

Mom sings her goofy songs.
"Tomorrow's a schoooool day,
schooooooool day!"
She takes my hand and we
Spin, Spin, Spin
around.

42

She pulls me in for a hug.
I squeeze her tight.
I feel her hair tickle my face.

"I love you, my little dinosaur," she says.
"Rawr" I whisper, and I squeeze her a little tighter.
And it calms my jitters down.

43

Other books by Lindsey Rowe Parker

About the Author

Lindsey Rowe Parker is the author of the award-winning book about sensory differences, *Wiggles, Stomps, and Squeezes Calm My Jitters Down*. A mom with a home full of neurodivergent minds, she is embracing the next phase of parenting while learning to navigate and advocate for her autistic daughter. With a recent adult diagnosis of ADHD, and a new deeper understanding of her own sensory experiences, she has begun to delve into the neurodiversity community, learning all she can from neurodivergent voices.

About the Illustrator

Rebecca Burgess is a comic artist and illustrator working in the UK, creating award-winning published and small press work. Along with drawing comics for their day job, Rebecca also loves drawing webcomics in their free time. Being autistic, they are particularly passionate about bringing more autistic characters into comics and stories! Outside of drawing comics and cuddling their cat, Rebecca also loves playing RPGs with friends, going on deep dives into history, and growing vegetables in their humble Bristol garden.